Docklands

for Martin and Filó

Docklands
A Ghost Story

Damian Walford Davies

Seren is the book imprint of
Poetry Wales Press Ltd.
57 Nolton Street, Bridgend, Wales, CF31 3AE
www.serenbooks.com
facebook.com/SerenBooks
twitter@SerenBooks

The right of Damian Walford Davies to be identified as
the author of this work has been asserted in accordance
with the Copyright, Designs and Patents Act, 1988.

ISBN: 978-1-78172-493-4
ebook: 978-1-78172-494-1
Kindle: 978-1-78172-495-8

A CIP record for this title is available from the British Library.

The publisher acknowledges the financial assistance of the Welsh Books Council.

Author photograph: Brychan Rhydderch Davies.

Printed in Bembo by Latimer Trend & Company Ltd, Plymouth.

Contents

House
September–December 1891

Fountain
January–May 1892

Commission

Cardiff,
August–November 1890

Perspective

From this gothic bay, flung out
above the hansoms

where O'Driscoll's pony
rests a ruined fetlock

on a backturned hoof,
I can see St Mary Street run plumb

until, a quarter-mile away,
it curves to kiss itself

beyond the French arcades.
I lead each client to this

balanced brink; instinctively,
they back away. *Revelation-*

thin, O'Driscoll's nag
evacuates the day in coarse, tan

gobs, heady sweetness
mixing with my new bay rum.

Firm

They're passable, as partners –
Prichard hidebound, wan,

unmacassared; Seddon fleshy,
soft-soaped by his wife,

able botcher of a country church;
both petted daft by flocks

of daughters, fond
of metaphors concerning bees;

temperate in everything
except the riot act

they read our Butetown lad
who grins and wrings the postbag

as he scans the ample camber
of our punters' wives

from bosom down to bustle.
Myself, I like the boy enormously.

Lecture

Their stipulations tickle me.
This Friday I address

St Mary's Mothers' Union
on that frothy text, 'The Architect

and God'. Mrs Aston's invitation
on the cream-wove paper,

blind-embossed, was breathless
as the messenger. Each month

I speak to guilds and schools,
but savour most the vestry's

chaste proximities. I can smell
each just-bathed body, each lavender-

dabbed wrist, the trail of scent
a woman draws from throat

to chest. *Ladies*, I'll begin; *I take
the swallow as my starting point.*

Salvage

Abercarn the godforsaken.
They asked me for a church;

what their blistered spirits
longed for was a monument

to firedamp and flood,
to bodies gaffed up black;

to those beyond the reach
of grappling hooks,

past even pity's plumbline...
So on the pediment

I gave them such a *pietà*! –
the son's dead heft

deposed along his mother's
knees, the cross and ladder

in the background conjuring
a headframe and the winding gear.

Spouse

Past ten, she has the desk lamp
in my study lit, *to lure me*

like a moth, she taunted,
home. Through the cedars

of Sophia Gardens,
I see the light prick darkness

like a spiteful eye. She meets me
on the landing, still in black –

gaunt hand resting on the newel post's
carved artichoke. Did I not also

hold the stillbirth in my palm
before they wrapped it in a pall

no bigger than my handkerchief?
I loathe her pallor,

hate the acrid odour
when I douse the lamp.

Villa

Lately, it's the house itself
that vexes her – each ornament

I drafted for her pleasure
now conjuring her loss. She scurries

past the little faces on the headstops –
sees the side wall's quoins

as rows of tiny caskets –
takes exception to my trademark

bead-and-reel as queerly
like her infant nephew's abacus –

jibs at how the bath-stone crosses
in the brick façade flush pink

at sundown...Damn it, woman –
while you're at it,

mock my copper flèche
and gilt acanthus balls.

Commission

The docklands brief: to level Angeline,
Louisa, Adelaide – ragtag terraces

of lean, abutting lives
from Wharf Street to the dun canal –

and raise a perfect square with limes
and fountains playing. It was me

all over, but they put it out to tender
out of tact. My pitch ran: *raze*

these breeding-grounds of vice
and vermin, bring our children

back into the light! It pleased
the dry bobs of the Temperance Brigade,

touched their lean wives' charitable
itch. Nights I wander crazy

Angeline and Adelaide, held up only
by the rigging of the washing lines.

Consumption

He says his young son's lungs
are shot, so I pay O'Driscoll triple

for our late-night rattle to the quays.
The Packet's best for beer. I watch,

between the cardsharps' shoulders,
shadow-play on curtains

in Louisa Street; then a deeper
square of black, like light, as someone

snuffs a candle. I lay my queens down
gently, with their dirty

chamfered edges curled.
Two girls, gartered, flank the fire –

versions of the mermaids
on the coat of arms they've carved

on Boston Buildings. Nipples
large and cold as father's shotgun slugs.

Thirst

On the drinking fountain
at the entrance to Bute Dock:

Stop, seaman! Take a draught —
there be danger fore and aft;

learn to shun that wicked craft
that smiles from yonder door.

The compass that is stationed here
will from danger keep you clear,

show you how to cox and steer
upon this dreadful shore.

Heed not the music and the sport
in alleyway or shadowed court;

they'll seduce you to a port
of rock and reef,

using you from stem to stern
to bring you, sailorman, to grief.

Fruit

In the Nonpareil Market –
windjammers' spars and masts

like winter copses
stretching out to sea behind the stalls –

I bought her oranges:
Spanish suns for grim Welsh skies.

The fish man with his barrow
full of ice now tips his cap

and grins; Mortlake the tobacconist
swaddles up my dozen

Flor de Dindigul cigars
in green tobacco leaves.

This quarter grows on me.
In shabby rooms in Stuart Street

my new friend swears
she'll tackle anything for oranges.

Girl

December 1890–March 1891

Solus

I was talking Bute Dock shares
in Atlas Chambers, Mr Maddocks'

sour-mash bourbon soused
in late bay light. From his velvet crow's nest

he can see his argosies
sail in from Mar del Plata, watch

his black hands caulk the keels
in dry docks' cribs. Off right,

my square was rising from the ruins
of the terraces. I saw her

through the whiskey's umber,
fractured by the lead-glass

tumbler's cuts: ten, or younger,
standing near my unbuilt fountain –

not exactly playing, all the greyer
for the glossy tarns of water at her feet.

Wives

Light tacks through loose
red rubble. I watched them

rope the final chimney stacks –
urban bellcotes with their cowled

red pots. The dustcloud
took all day to clear; its tang –

now sweet, now acrid –
conjured last night's staged

saltpetre smoke that veiled
the cheap illusionist's *hey prestos*

with his wasted wife
in Queen's Street Theatre.

At home, she met me ashen
at the bottom of the stairwell,

raised a finger; licked it;
marked a cheerless kiss on my lapel.

Trade

I woke, guts roiling, at eleven,
her mint infusion sickly

on the tongue. Her tears
had made the cheap ink

of the *Argus* run. This time
it was ten lewd column inches

on the back-room quack
caught grubbing tiny lives

from rounding bellies – postscripts
buried at the river end of Ely wood.

He'll hang. I headed for a trim,
returned all nicks and styptic.

My lawyer's fond of quoting *Punch*:
Some are born barbers;

other men have barberism
rudely thrust upon them.

Saw

I was in The Packet's parlour
with our dandy Clerk of Works,

toasting our foundation stone –
my name carved deep

in stark sans-serif. We were
on our fourth French brandy

when they lugged a docker
screaming through a side door

in a sail – his crushed and cockeyed peg
appalling. From nowhere,

someone set to work:
knifestrokes, sawstrokes, reef knot

to the artery, and the grey girl
watching from the far side

of the room, indifferent
as they let the waste leg go.

Warp, Weft

I called the new maid back.
She halted as if struck, breakfast china

trembling on the tray. Eighteen,
perhaps, and oh so plain. *What's that?*

I asked her, pointing to the wall.
Ma'am's sampler, sir, she stuttered,

bobbing like a river bird. It was
unremarkable – tendrilled border,

doggerel, geometric Christmas trees
in listless symmetries, culled

from sober pattern books – except
those two outlandish icons, wholly hers:

a hooded cradle, dark inside;
and opposite, a girl, her body's stitches

fraying. My morning souchong
tasted black and bitter in the throat.

Ceremony

The Hon. Laetitia Ashdown
botched the cutting of the ribbon

barring entry to my finished school
(a brash *pro bono* essay on –

how shall I...? – the *suburban
Romanesque*). She hacked and slashed

until I took the blunted scissors
from her, bit the crimson strip

and ripped my building open
to perplexed applause. On the breeze,

a tang of sea, of salt, that brought
the girl insistently to mind;

I stood there stupid with the civic
shears, searching for her

till the Hon. Laetitia Ashdown,
blushing, prised them from my hand.

Reflections

In lengthening March light
I watched them coax the low walls

closer to a mortared clinch.
Tramping out, they stacked their hods

against dark tors of sand
like castoff crutches at a shrine.

I'd watched for her all day,
primed for greyness at the edges

of the mind. I was on the spot
where she'd been standing

gazing up at me. I spun to Atlas
Chambers, half expecting her;

the panes were blind. I stirred
the rainpools with my cane;

they offered nothing but
a flashing darkness back.

Bestiary

I was there to cheer the follies
on the castle wall:

vulture, seal, beaver, imbecile
bear. Bravo the mad hyena! –

beefy snarler, hackles up,
scrabbling at the parapet

as the brass band played
The Man Who Broke the Bank

at Monte Carlo. A Lottie Collins
lookalike swanked on to shriek

Ta-ra-ra boom-de-aye
in a wicked Cockney drawl.

The beasts observed the party
from their heartless

height. I'd seen the lynx's
deadpan stare before.

Decadent

Yesterday from London, draped
in yellow silk: *Lippincott's*

from last July – the one with
Mr Wilde's dark parable

of Dorian Gray. I read it brazenly
at chambers, left its scarlet masthead

in the open as a lure.
She came to me this evening

in her hunger, stepping
with a rustle out of mourning,

thin and alabaster – pressed herself
against me till my watch chain

printed patterns on her breasts.
I gripped her by the shoulders, gauged

my strength against her birdlike
frame. She looked so sickeningly old.

Chattel

I was chatting to O'Driscoll
when his horse fell dead. Curious:

slamming to its knees, bone
spearing through the skin,

it hung there in full harness,
rank waste pouring down its legs.

A small crowd brewed.
Then *he* was down, pawing

at the shabby flank. His beast's bass
groan and rattle made them all

step back. In my rooms, cognac
brought out harder tears.

I slipped him something
from our petty cash

and asked about his boy.
He hugged his shins and howled.

Square

April–August 1891

Butcher's

Scraping black conserve on slips
of toast, she called my bluff:

I'll come to see your square.
When she stepped out to the street

her mourning had a green-blue sheen
it hadn't boasted in the half-light

of the house. Down Bute East
the chestnut bay plunged sideways,

pitched her, glossy, into me.
She smoothed her bombazine

hysterically. *Home,* she shouted,
Home! I couldn't say for sure,

but she must have seen her, framed
by Klimaszewski's rows of game –

the child again, reaching out to us,
eyes sightless as the bloody hares'.

Flora

So she spoke at last. I was watching
Powell's pleasure steamers

trouble one another's wakes
across the bay. Something touched

my cuff. She was twenty feet away,
already turning for the saltings

where the carcass of the *Hamadryad*,
crammed with sailors'

sickbeds, lies like Noah's ark.
I followed, asked her name.

Em, she whispered, breaking
stems of glasswort, forked

and knobbed like chickens' feet.
There were bruises, yellowing

round their plum and lilac hearts.
She gave a brackish smile.

Migrants

I was watching martins
solder grey, impastoed nests

between the bargeboards
and the settled walls.

My square was chirruping
with revenants. She took my hand,

halting underneath the half-built
tabernacles – told me

how her mother swears a house
that hosts such twittering

is fortunate all year. She led me
to the west side's empty eaves.

To pedal notes from Bristol packets
off the bay, she blithely sang:

Madame Martlet won't raise young
Where some mischief has been done.

Interior

They were papering the parlours
on the west side of the square —

alternating lilac, yellow, green
from house to house along the line

of old Louisa Street. I got jawing
with a cocksure 'prentice, busy

slapping glue in thick cream gobs
along a length of roll. Sliding on

the last barred strip, he offered:
Wasn' i' by 'ere tha' fucker Foley

lived? I 'opes he took 'is time
to croak. He smoothed the paper

lovingly, the brush's tawny lashes
curling off the wall. He'd missed

a bubble. I fought an urge
to prick it with my pen.

Opening

They'd commandeered a chamber
in the Coal Exchange, tricked it out

in flowers from Crockherbtown's
cottage gardens. She'd sloughed off

black, entering electric on my arm –
gauze sleeves filtering the light.

Furred husbands fawned on her –
Ah, Eleanor! So good to see you

*out...*Above a silver salver's image
of the coffered roof, I quizzed

the Crime Commissioner on Foley
and Louisa Street. A toast came booming

from the dais: Atlantic Square!
Ah, vile, he answered; *five, six years ago,*

perhaps – a child. His own...
Atlantic Square! I echoed, mindlessly.

Spectrum

I led Lord Bute towards the camera.
Someone vanished

underneath its velvet pall. We posed
beside my mermaid fountain

in a crushing civic grip. Ragging
him, I said my fishy girl

was modelled on a late Etruscan bronze.
He smirked. A valve was turned

and water slicked her flesh
to gloved applause. And then I swear

I saw the girl – clawing at a bedroom
window, screaming dumb

behind the white jet's rainbow
mist. *I'm not a bloody fool. You took*

those great slack breasts – he leered –
that belly crease, from life, you fox.

Bouquet

She smells the docks and all
on me. I say I may indeed

have spent the evening talking Paris,
ships and Norway churches

with my good friend Mr Dahl
and anyway, what of it,

now her mind is black again –
busy burying itself

beneath the little swelling in the turf
her endless laying on of lilies

simply flattens to the level
of all loss? *Still no stone,*

she sobs; *it's beastly, cruel.*
She sniffs me like a bitch,

picturing the wearer
of the brassy wharfside scent.

Dessert

She sat there mum, on sufferance,
Mrs Dahl's arpeggio laughter

ringing off the faceted decanters,
the table candelabra's

teardrop glass. Through a fug of port
I watched the candles' wicks

feed ever-thinner cypresses of flame
that sputtered tongues of soot,

listened to the world rasp gorgeously
in Mrs Dahl's French throat.

You're a lucky man,
Herr Dahl, I offered,

as a mawkish muscatel came round.
She flinched, left untouched

her goat's cheese
with its speckled coat of ash.

Tea

Mr Enos Royston, Francophile,
scuttles out to Duke Street's boulevard,

linen apron double-tied,
to rearrange his wicker chairs

and café tables. He's a huckster
like the others, but he touts with style,

coaxing strollers from the street
to take their oolong under gluey limes

that filter light like fine stained glass.
My silver ball infuser gave out

rusty puffs of tea. I saw the infant boy
cracked sideways by the flouncing mare,

the mother's scream freeze Enos
arching over with the sugar tongs – so close

I read the bonewhite buttons
on his waistcoat: *Cardin, France.*

Vesper

I'm fêted in the journals, my name
the latest slang for how to make stone

swank. The Square is working hard
for me. Out of habit now,

I take an evening jaunt down Harrowby
to watch the clippers clot

to tar-black silhouettes against the sun.
I'd forgotten her, but yesterday

in failing light, where Hunter Street
concedes to belts of shale, I saw her

on the far dock wall, listing windward
like a pallid figurehead.

I started flapping up a hectic semaphore,
my half-unrigged companion slurring:

Lover — wha' you wavin' at?
Treacle, wha' d'you see?

House

September–December 1891

Play

They've dug a line of pits
along Cathedral Road –

sumps of dark that late September
clogs with sodden leaves.

This evening, from the room
she calls the nursery,

I watch them rig and raise
three gaslamps – regulation stems

but fetching swan-neck ironwork
below the visored hoods.

When the gas jet's fired
and the mantles glow,

perhaps the light will play
across these walls,

casting shadows of her
dandling nothing on her knees.

Trail

Back – unusually – at four,
I tracked the tang of oranges

from hallway through to library
and drawing-room and up

across the landing
where my sixteen-light clerestory

pools lozenges of sun
on custom-fired tiles,

to find her in our bedroom,
flushed and frigging,

and the smack of Seville ceding
to a gagging stench that faded

as I watched her fingers
tuck a wayward curl

behind her ear, smooth
her dark embarrassment of skirts.

O

I was on the walnut ladder
in the library, looking

for the Richter brothers' tome
on tower clocks, when the evening

lost its savour and a blackness
bloomed inside me like a gob

of blotted ink. I turned to see her
gibbous on the margin

of the streetlamp's ring of light,
glaring at the window of the nursery

a floor above, mouth open
in a gross, dark O.

Em? I whispered at the pane,
my own breath clouding her.

Later at my desk, I drew the clockface
of the new asylum blank and black.

Visitation

They sent a downy
lisping little shit to tell me

that my square's north side
was shear-line shot

and listing out of true.
I asked him how he came to be

a connoisseur of cracks.
He wasn't drawn.

It was then I saw the child
pass fast across the doorjamb,

bare knees beetroot-red.
Who let her in? I shouted

to an empty stairwell.
I rang the bell. He passed me

smirking, peeling on
a gallous pair of gloves.

Rime

I watched her hanging
six-inch lengths of lard

on scarlet ribbons
from the garden's holly trees.

She'd spent the morning
rolling them in millet seed

until her palms were glib.
For the little birds,

she whispered, ribbons ranged
like gashes on her wrists.

I counted fifteen
of her sallow tapers blurring

in her freezing breath; by four
they wore a sheath of frost.

She might as well have strung up
scarecrows. No birds came.

Nocturne

I woke to a dark I could taste,
the fire out, Spiridion & Son's

new timepiece striking tinny
from the castle tower, hour

and echo bleeding. I lay there
thinking of the two bright pennies

and the walnut shells
they place in winter on the pendulum

to make contracting metal
keep good time. The cold

was ferric in the lungs.
I wrapped the counterpane

around me like a stole
and went to her, slipped inside

my body's furrow in the mattress
as if it were another self.

Unto us

She'd dressed the Christmas tree
with candles, child-faced redcoats

hanging by their shakos, slices
of dried orange spiked with cloves.

In the baubles' hall of mirrors
I was watching how my smoke rings

seemed to bend behind me
in the bloated room.

Then gladness leached away;
in the burnished silver balls

I saw the girl squat near the fire
screaming, bloodied, begging

somebody to stop. I didn't turn
to face her, only later breaking

when I saw how like so many tiny femurs
were the brownblack sticks of cloves.

Siren

I knew then. We found ourselves
together in the drawing room,

listening over fine bone china's
cant and single pots of tea

to two weeks' worth of water
streaming down the thick-slashed throats

of *Evans, Cardiff*'s patent iron grilles.
We'd left the colour wheel

of pastel Paris macarons
inviolate. She turned to me

and started singing – all air
and sibilants, then loud

against the culverts' gutturals –
a song that named the girl

and called her in to where
she found us ready, holding hands.

Periphrastic

I sent a boy to dredge O'Driscoll
from St Mary Street, tracked him

on the hairsbreadth finger of my watch
up Quay Street with its ziggurats of dung

past ranks of gartered ladybirds
on Womanby to Westgate,

where he turned his breakneck
cab-and-nag and with a bobbing

sprig of ling between the horse's ears,
drew up like a hearse. I pussyfooted,

spoke in parables: *the docklands stray —
the Packet waif and glasswort girl —*

*my little mam'selle martlet —
hamadryad Em*...He shrank back

on his box. *Dead Em Foley walks,*
he said, the horror keener for his brogue.

À deux

I asked her if she cared to dress
to see the new year in. As she fixed

my neck-tie with her father's lapis pin,
I caught her wedding scent,

rose otto, on her wrists. I fumbled
with her cobweb choker's catch

until she turned and fastened it herself.
Akimbo elbows push the breasts up

high. In the hall, the cook was busy leaving,
inefficiently; thrown, she watched us,

lockstep, turn the dog-leg hand–in–hand.
Sitting down to spatchcock

with their blistered stumps, we knew
a third was in the room. We waited with her

for the mantel chimes that bring
a new year like a foundling to the door.

Fountain

January–May 1892

Gauge

She's our hearts' barometer:
a week Set Fair between us

and she's silent. Our bickering
brings her keening back.

When I dream of dirty fingernails
and orange peel in jigsaw pieces

in a dockside room, she wakes us
with her screams. And still

the maid's clasped diary
notes nothing but the daily round.

I read the Foley trial – lay it loose-leaf
on the pink-wash elevations

on my drafting board. It hammers home
Louisa Street, Louisa Street. I build

as well as ever, conjure her in faces
carved as corbels on Cathedral Road.

Cemetery

The gardener knew her;
so did a woman scraping gullshit

with a bassine brush
from marble anchor flukes

and angels' hems. She left
the path, led me criss-cross

through the plots
to where we'd watched a box

no bigger than her jewel case
let down as if it had some

weight. She mouthed his name;
I stammered it. At home,

the girl there with us,
I heard myself say: *See,*

I brush my small son's
gravesoil from my spats.

Gifts

Some days my mermaid fountain
in Atlantic Square unsettles me –

how her tapered skirt of fishscales
cedes to ruffled bellyskin, how I made her

spew those streams of sloggering
dock water over her own face

until, in last month's northerlies,
she blurred inside a chrysalis of ice.

We walk together now, each evening,
in the holm oak avenue behind the house

where the thaw's allowed the jays
to rootle for last autumn's acorns,

cached in pits. As we pass,
they bicker in the branches, flares

of pink and black-barred turquoise
sending showers down like little pentecosts.

Stole

St Mary Street was dogged with gulls
the squalls had driven in. When they call,

their gape lays bare a shocking
tongue. I picked my way through brutes

as big as buzzards to the Royal Arcade.
I'd seen a red Manila shawl on show

in Bentinck's – beaded, deep-fringed,
thick with lion-dogs and roses –

for her birthday gift. Haloed by his name
in gold-leaf letters on the plate-glass pane,

Erasmus Bentinck – *trained at Bloomingdale's* –
slid it off the black wire mannequin,

twirled it like a mad gonfalonier
to make the fabric dance. Behind him

in the stream of shoppers stood the girl.
She hugged herself as if the shawl were hers.

Figure

I'd finished off a chapel
for the Weston Methodists,

ragging them with hints of Hawksmoor
and some wanton puns on Wren.

From my bay, I watched St Mary Street
reviving after rain. Woken by the sun,

O'Driscoll shifted in his oilskin
at the cab-stand; his bowler

held the morning's downpour
in its rim. I rapped the pane;

he raised his face; the bright ring
sluiced off in a flashing plait.

At the drafting board,
I sketched a figure for a fountain –

water jetting up around her, copper-
cast, mid-jeté, bleeding verdigris.

Cross-section

She let her dress stream off,
stepped across the dark blue moat

around her feet. As if along
a corridor of long-barred doors,

she tacked towards me,
the lamp behind her

moving in and out of curt
eclipse. There was a shift of scale:

as if I'd opened up the frontage
of a doll's house, I saw us from outside:

tiny figures coming to a clinch;
cook and maid above us

in their matchbox beds; and in the attic
where, one baying Saturday,

I'd set it down and locked it
rocking in the dark, a crib.

Recipe

Spring's promised even to the saltings,
where the coal-dust tide lugs in

to melt the ice-crust in the courses,
then to freeze again. O'Driscoll showed me

samphire sleeping in its woody stems.
His dead boy foraged with him

for the bright green shoots.
Good to munch on, boiled and slick

with butter come July, he said, or thick
with scallions in a salty champ.

I could taste it in his eyes. Behind him
at the dockside staithes, men sprang

on trucks like bantam devils in a Doom.
Jim, I said; *come now, don't cry* –

my awkward naming given music
by the sounding of a two-tone channel buoy.

Waist

Today she slipped the sheets again
and blundered out to retch. Behind the door,

the tassels on her dressing gown
kept time like pendulums.

The cistern emptied twice,
the system shutting with a shrill

intake of breath. She slid back in
to bed, held the coverlet in fistfuls

at her chin. *She's gone*, she said,
I think she's gone. Light clarified

like Jim O'Driscoll's butter in a pan.
Around the house, I notice

how her right hand haunts her belly
where the boning on her bodice

shows like ribs. The waist's all waspish
for her leg-of-mutton sleeves.

Nereid

We watched them hoist my mermaid
from her plinth, laying bare the pipe

that kinked inside her curves.
Faces mobbed the windows

in Atlantic Square. They wrapped her
in an oilskin, beached her in a wagon

where she seemed to thrash and writhe.
Bute's navvies laboured at the pedestal,

cutting, twisting, making good.
From a shroud of gunny cloth they drew

Em Foley, winched her up to fix her
leaping seaward, tiny petrels

playing round her heels.
Doors opened. The square came out

to recognise a dead girl risen, riding
seaspray, bruises turned to gold.

Return

The Companies' May banquet
finished with a Rayne Vigneau sauterne –

a vintage lost on lean marine insurers
and their voided-velvet wives.

I was stone cold sober, gifting them
a speech on Stanford White's basilica

at Lovely Lane in Baltimore, patterned
on Pomposa, Italy. They all looked blank.

I woke the Mayor, mouthed
'worshipful' until it sounded like a slur

and was the first to leave. At the bridge,
two mudlarks grabbed my deep-forked

coat-tails, called me *swallow, swallow*;
I gave them pocket-pence. They left me

at Sophia Gardens, where I saw
she'd had my study lit to light me home.

Note

Docklands emerges from a long fascination with buildings, ground, maps and the dead.

I began the book as a way of helping me to understand and bed down in a new city – a way of finding, in all senses, a living.

Maps old and new became guides I used to conjure and walk the world of the volume's architect-speaker. They brought home to me how our present environments are ghosted by – and merely overlay – past incarnations. If anyone should be able to understand that, it is an architect.

Fieldwork was crucial, too. I took to exploring 'docklands' (that now strange amalgam of Mermaid Quay, Cardiff Bay, Tiger Bay, the Barrage, Butetown and Bristol Channel vistas...) and the well-to-do Cathedral Road area of west Cardiff where the architect and his wife reside in a newly built villa (self-designed, self-reflecting).

I started to view stereoscopically: seeing coal staithes and railway sidings where there are now bars and burger restaurants; O'Driscoll's cab-stand in St Mary Street where Friday-night queues for nightclubs stretch back from bomber-jacketed bouncers; fleets of trading ships in the bay where now sedate pleasure-craft ply designated routes across a sweet-water lagoon; a shadow in James Street near the estate agent's and the Irie Shack. Often it was the modern city that gave face and form to my Victorian world: David Nathan's sculpture, *Nereid* (1995–6), in the Kingsway gave me elements of 'Dead Em Foley'.

We have only the architect's word(s) for it. I was troubled at first by the ambiguous identity of 'she' and 'her' across the poems (his wife? the girl? his docklands ladies?), but I now hope that the indistinctness reflects an aspect of his teetering and layered world.

Always, the ghost comes with a smack of salt, guilt with a tang of orange.

Acknowledgements

Thanks are due to the editors of the following publications, where some of the poems in this volume first appeared: *Agenda, Barrow Street, Planet: The Welsh Internationalist, Poetry Wales* and *The World is Charged: Poetic Engagements with Gerard Manley Hopkins*, ed. Daniel Westover and William Wright (Clemson University Press, 2016).

I am grateful to Francesca Rhydderch, John Barnie, Richard Marggraf Turley, Kevin Mills and Amy Wack for their insight and advice on how to manage the ghostly; and to Peter Finch, deep mapper of Cardiff's strata.

About the Author

Damian Walford Davies was born in Aberystwyth in 1971. He has published three previous collections with Seren – *Suit of Lights* (2009), *Witch* (2012) and *Judas* (2015) – and has also edited a collection of R. S. Thomas's poems – *Poems for Elsi* (2013) – for Seren. His other poetry books include the co-written *Whiteout* (2006), a pamphlet, *Alabaster Girls* (2015), and the forthcoming poem-libretto, *The Mare's Tale*. He is Pro Vice-Chancellor and Head of the College of Arts, Humanities and Social Sciences at Cardiff University. He lives in Cardiff. He believes, some days, in ghosts.

Also by Damian Walford Davies

'crackles with intelligence and inventiveness...a performer with great panache and stylistic verve.'
— Nicholas Murray, *Planet: The Welsh Internationalist*

'wittily judged. The diction pulses with the power of different registers and the accompanying emotional gear-changes are psychologically satisfying. Above all, there is a musical rightness...'
— John Redmond, *New Welsh Review*

'Astonishing, knock-you-backwards work...startlingly different.'
— Jane Holland, www.handstar.co.uk

'tender, shocking, playful, sharp-eyed — a suitably sparkling performance.'
— Caroline Clark, *Gwales*

'His lines startle with freshness and animation...hung like notes of music...refined, but never squeamish...encompass[ing] modern mess and myth...not decorative, but keenly political...outstanding...'
— Alison Brackenbury

'Verse with content that stretches the ways to write...we need more like this.'
— Peter Finch, peterfinchpoet.blogspot.com

'as colourfully dramatic in its way as The Crucible…an unsettling and original masterpiece.'
— Bernard O'Donoghue

'masterly.'
— Alice Entwistle, *Poetry Wales*

'Richly detailed and engrossing…vividly imaginative and intelligent.'
— Jane Yeh, *New Welsh Review*

'brooding…fascinating and deeply unsettling…an irresistible narrative drive.'
— Laura Wainwright, *www.walesartsreview.org*

'A remarkable work, at once poetic sequence, play and novel…the poems crackle with emotion and brilliantly evoke time and place…like Arthur Miller and Carol Churchill, this artist continues to understand, depict and warn.'
— Caroline Clark, *Gwales*

'...*teases us with a collision of registers and of historical moments...
highly suggestive and moving...beautifully crafted...it explores alternative
representations of Judas, whose voice also speaks for the marginalised or
silenced.*'
— Justin Jones, *Wales Arts Review*

'...*exciting...a dynamic journey...a brilliant and unique collection from
an acclaimed poet, its subject matter bringing alive ambiguities and moral
questions from the past and present.*'
— Clare Owen-Maynard, *Gwales*

'*An apocryphal* tour de force. *With dazzling linguistic precision,
mordant wit and unflinching humanity, these poems turn the familiar
story inside out, exposing how the veil between past and present, love and
betrayal, magic and miracle is fine, and easily torn.*'
— Tiffany Atkinson